THE GOSPEL OF GRACE

Why Do So Many Leaders Refuse to Preach it?

THE GOSPEL OF GRACE

Why Do So Many Leaders Refuse to Preach it?

JEREMIAH JOHNSON

I lovingly dedicate this book to all the Sauls that will become Pauls

FOREWORD

When Jesus trailblazed, his world-changing three-and-a-half-year ministry on earth, he was fiercely celebrated by the common people as a hero. The sinners would come out in droves to see him. Without television, without radio, without social media or the internet, the fame of Jesus spread like wildfire across the land. Crowds literally thronged him wherever he went. Tax collectors climbed trees, people ripped roofs off houses, children sang songs and placed palms in the streets. It's no secret that Jesus was wildly popular. However, Jesus was not popular with everyone. There was a smaller, more powerful, more influential group that quite literally hated him.

The religious leaders of the day, the scribes, the Pharisees, and the Sadducees, spent most of their time and energy conspiring to kill him. The more popular Jesus became, the more their jealousy and hatred grew. Jesus' revolutionary message struck a warm endearing chord in the hearts of the people and simultaneously challenged the gross hypocrisy of the religious leaders of the day. The Pharisees and Sadducees had the titles and positions, they had the power and influence, they had the best seats in the synagogues, they knew how to "have church," but their hearts had grown cold to a real relationship with God.

Jesus came preaching a message of freedom and genuine relationship with God. Suddenly, the religious hierarchy was challenged. The people were responding to the easy yoke of Jesus and rejecting the heavy yoke of the scribes and Pharisees. Jesus was, is, and always will be a revolutionary. The deep-seated desire in the heart of man to know, and ultimately please his creator, has been hurtfully manipulated by those that want to be in control for hundreds of years. Our enemy takes his best shots when he is posing as something that is good.

As it was then, so it is now. We are currently experiencing a worldwide reformation in the body of Christ toward Jesus and his amazing grace. For far too long we have heard graceless sermons filled with man-centered efforts that give a discreet nod toward Jesus but don't glorify and honor him as savior. We have heard so many mixed messages of old and new covenant, law and grace, that the church has been in a state of confusion concerning who they are and who God is. We have had people begin to almost worship spiritual leaders and their works more than Jesus and his finished work on the cross. In the absence of grace man-made religion always begins to form.

Yet, God has a plan to break the church free from man-made religious chains and bring our focus back to Jesus. God has a plan to restore these leaders whose minds have been blinded to amazing grace. Every Saul is one donkey slip away from becoming a Paul. Join me as we take a look at the lives of a few different leaders in scripture who struggled with a religious mindset.

I believe this will help us understand why many modern-day leaders reject the message of the gospel of grace. As we take this journey together, my prayer is that these insights will birth compassion and hope toward these leaders. God loves them and he has a plan of redemption for their lives.

CHAPTER 1

LOOKING THROUGH THE LENS OF THE CROSS

I WOULD LIKE to begin by asking you to please understand as your read, a large portion of this book consists of teaching from the Old Testament, through the lens of New Testament concepts. While the story of Jonah took place under the old covenant, we are under a new covenant now. Jesus changed everything. However, this doesn't mean that we throw the Old Testament out of our Bibles.

2 Timothy 3:16–17 says,

All Scripture is given by inspiration of God, and is profitable for doctrine, for reproof, for correction, for instruction in righteousness, that the man of God may be complete, thoroughly equipped for every good work.

That includes the Old Testament scriptures as well. We do an injustice to ourselves to think we must throw out more than half the Bible because we are no longer under the old covenant. There are great truths and tremendous gems of wisdom in these scriptures. In the New Testament, Jesus is revealed; in the Old Testament Jesus was concealed. He was hidden for us to discover as the Holy Spirit illuminates those scriptures to gloriously reveal the son of God.

The true nature and plan of God was concealed in the old covenant and then revealed in Jesus in the new covenant. Jesus came saying, "If you've seen me, you have seen the Father." If you want to see what Father God is truly like, you can look at Jesus. Jesus came helping people and loving people. We see this clearly in Acts 10:38.

How God anointed Jesus of Nazareth with the Holy Spirit and with power, and he went about doing good and healing all who were oppressed by the devil, for God was with him.

Jesus never broke anyone's leg to teach them something, he never called down fire to destroy his enemies, he never laid hands on someone and gave them leprosy. Jesus went around doing good, healing and helping people. Jesus revealed to the entire world that the true nature of his Father was love. Jesus did something that the law and the prophets could never do. Jesus revealed to the world that God was love and he wanted to save the world, not condemn it.

Hebrews 10:1 says,

For the law, having a shadow of the good things to come, and not the very image of the things…

If you see the shadow of my hand, you can learn many things about my hand—the shape, the size, the fact that it's a hand. However, if you see the image of my actual hand, you will see the color of my skin, the details of fingernails and hair. The picture will now be full and clear. The Old Testament was a shadow of the truth; the New Testament is the image of that truth in the face of Jesus Christ.

So, as we look closely at these Old Testament scriptures, we must ask, and allow the Holy Spirit to lead us and see everything through the filter of the cross. We must look at everything through Jesus and his finished work, revealing the full picture from the shadow we are looking at.

There are all kinds of beautiful jewels of wisdom in the Bible's pages but we must filter everything through the cross as we study it. Let me give you an example where Paul does this. In Galatians chapter 4 Paul uses two figures out of the Old Testament to represent the concepts of law and grace.

Galatians 4:21-26

Tell me, you who desire to be under the law, do you not hear the law? For it is written that Abraham had two sons: the one by a bondwoman, the other by a freewoman. But he who was of the bondwoman was born according to the flesh, and he of the freewoman through promise, which things are symbolic. For these are the two covenants: the one from Mount Sinai, which gives birth to bondage, which is Hagar—for this Hagar is Mount Sinai in Arabia, and corresponds to Jerusalem which now is, and is in bondage with her children—but the Jerusalem above is free, which is the mother of us all.

We can see clearly that Paul, through the inspiration of the Holy Spirit, goes back to Old Testament scriptures to bring forth New Testament concepts that bless us with wisdom. We will periodically be doing the same thing in this book. So, as I go through these scriptures I'm not going to be able to constantly stop and explain the difference between the old and new covenant, even though, as a grace preacher, I will want to, so I'm going to do it once, here, at the beginning of this book.

CHAPTER 2

UNGRACIOUS JONAH

The story of Jonah is a remarkable exchange between God and one of his ministers. God comes to Jonah and tells him to preach a message to the city of Nineveh.

Jonah 1:1 says,

Now the word of the Lord came to Jonah the son of Amittai, saying, "Arise, go to Nineveh, that great city, and cry out against it; for their wickedness has come up before me."

It was not unusual for God to call his ministers to preach a message to a group of people, but what was unusual was Jonah's reaction to God asking him to preach this message.

Jonah 1:3

But Jonah arose to flee to Tarshish from the presence of the Lord. He went down to Joppa, and found a ship going to Tarshish; so he paid the fare, and went down into it, to go with them to Tarshish from the presence of the Lord.

Instead of responding with excitement and enthusiasm to preach this message, Jonah refuses to preach it, and immediately runs away—very strange behavior to say the least. I'm sure most of you are very familiar with what happens next: there have been many songs and children's books written about Jonah in the belly of the whale. However, what is not often talked about is why Jonah refused to preach this message. Why did Jonah run from the presence of God? We don't find out why until the beginning of chapter 4.

Jonah 4:1

But it displeased Jonah exceedingly, and he became angry. So he prayed to the Lord, and said, "Ah, Lord, was not this what I said when I was still in my country? Therefore I fled previously to Tarshish; for I know that You are a gracious and merciful God, slow to anger and abundant in lovingkindness, One who relents from doing harm. Therefore now,

O Lord, please take my life from me, for it is better for me to die than to live!"

Jonah knew God was gracious, merciful, slow to anger, abundant in loving-kindness, and one who relents from doing harm; Jonah knew God had a plan to save these people, not harm them.

Why in the world would a preacher be more excited about destroying people than saving them? Nineveh was renowned for its cruelty and violence, even by the standards of that time. It was common practice to skin the rulers of kingdoms that opposed them and hang those human skins on the walls of their temples. These guys were a special kind of wicked.

We can kind of deduce through the passage of scripture that Jonah seems to know if he preaches the message that God gave him for this city that these people will change, but he doesn't want them to change; he wants them to "get what they deserve." Inside of Jonah there seems to be a real sense of justice that wants to be appeased. Jonah wasn't ready for these people to just get off scot-free, so to speak. Jonah was offended at God's graciousness. Jonah wanted them to be punished.

Jonah refused to be the vessel that God's grace flowed through, because deep inside of Jonah he didn't think it was fair. Many times, our concepts of fairness and God's concepts of fairness can be two totally different things. Many times, the religious mindset has a twisted sense of vindictive justice, predisposed to a sense of self-righteous self-exaltation while condemning others. It's a very wicked thing and it in no way accurately represents the heart of Father God.

A very clear example of the contrast between the heart of God and the mindset of religion is with the woman caught in the act of adultery. The Pharisees and Sadducees had been hearing Jesus preach these messages of God's graciousness toward sinners and God's judgement toward the self-righteous. They wanted to push Jesus into a position where he had to judge and punish a sinner or be forced to violate the integrity of the law. They were trying to trap him. Jesus masterfully represents the gracious heart of the Father and simultaneously upholds the integrity of the law.

First, Jesus removes her condemners by knocking over the self-righteous footstool they were standing on, condemning her from. He says, "You that are without sin cast the first stone." He removes the law as a moral platform for them to stand on and condemn others from, then he points the law at them. They all dropped their stones and left as their consciences convicted them under the proper use of the law.

Jesus was left standing before her, he who had never sinned, so he had a right to judge this woman and cast the first stone. However, instead of condemning her, Jesus reveals the gracious heart of the Father instead. God doesn't want to destroy this woman, he wants to save her from the sin that is destroying her. Jesus forgives her and encourages her not to sin again. Man-made religion's sense of self-righteous, vindictive justice, is confounded.

We see a similar type of attitude try to crop up in Jesus' disciples during his earthly ministry. We find Jesus and his disciples on their way to Jerusalem, and as they are on this journey they need a place to stop and rest along the way. The disciples go ahead of Jesus and find a Samaritan town for them to stay in. The people in the town refuse to let them stay when they find out that Jesus is just stopping in for the night on his way to Jerusalem. The disciples are furious at this insulting injustice. Their response is, "Hey, let's call fire down and kill these guys." The disciples are ready to settle this account like a bad Clint Eastwood movie. We pick up the story in Luke 9:51:

Now it came to pass, when the time had come for Him to be received up, that He steadfastly set His face to go to Jerusalem, and sent messengers before His face. And as they went, they entered a village of the Samaritans, to prepare for Him. But they did not receive Him, because His face was set for the journey to Jerusalem. And when His disciples James and John saw this, they said, "Lord, do You want us to command fire to come down from heaven and consume them, just as Elijah did?"

But He turned and rebuked them, and said, "You do not know what manner of spirit you are of. For the Son of Man did not come to destroy men's lives but to save them." And they went to another village.

Jesus responds with a rebuke to the disciples, saying you don't quite yet understand the heart of God: we are not here to destroy people, we are here to save people.

There is something inside of man's heart that cries for justice, but many times God's sense of justice and our sense of justice is completely different. Sometimes we want people to "get what they deserve." We have a sense of "fairness" that many times is diametrically opposed to the heart of God.

In Hebrews 12:24 it says,

to Jesus the Mediator of the new covenant, and to the blood of sprinkling that speaks better things than that of Abel.

Abel's blood cried out for revenge. Jesus' blood cries out for forgiveness. Both are cries of justice but one is a higher level of justice than the first.

There is a marked difference in the way things are handled in the old and new covenant. The new covenant more clearly represents the heart of God, whereas the old covenant addressed and satisfied man's sense of justice. "An eye for eye, and a tooth for a tooth." A sense of fairness was achieved through justice being meted out according to short accounts between fellowman on earth. Is that justice? Absolutely. But there would eventually come a higher justice when Jesus arrived on the scene. Jesus settled everyone's petty accounts by paying the price for everyone's transgression. On the cross Jesus received the condemnation against sin in his flesh.

In 2 Corinthians 5:21 it says,

For He made Him who knew no sin to be sin for us, that we might become the righteousness of God in Him.

It was the great exchange, but, it was completely unfair in our sense of justice. The lamb who took away the sins of the world never sinned. He never transgressed and yet he was treated as the worse sinner who ever lived. He became one with our sin so we could become one with his righteousness.

In Hebrews 2:9 it says,

But we see Jesus, who was made a little lower than the angels, for the suffering of death crowned with glory and honor, that He, by the grace of God, might taste death for everyone.

By grace Jesus received something he did not deserve, death, so we could receive something we did not deserve, everlasting life. Grace trumps and supersedes man's sense of justice with a greater gift than we could ever imagine. At its core grace is an unmerited, undeserved favor; grace reveals the goodness of God even in the midst of our failure and disobedience. The impact is, grace causes us to fall in love with God and it's his goodness that leads us to repentance rather than just the fear of punishment.

When Jonah gets the message from God to preach to these horrible, immoral people in the city of Nineveh, Jonah is really upset, because he knows God is gracious and merciful and has a desire to save these people rather than give them "what they deserve." Sometimes the goodness of God can offend the sense of justice in man.

Another great example of this is the parable of the eleventh-hour worker. Jesus regularly gave parables to help us understand what God's kingdom is like. In the parable, the first-hour workers agree with the landowner to work all day for one day's wages. As the day progresses the landowner hires the eleventh-hour worker, who works only one hour.

When it's time for everyone to get paid, the landowner pays the eleventh-hour worker first and pays them a full day's wages. When it's time for the first-hour worker to get paid they think they will receive more because they worked all day. They in turn are given a full day's wages and they begin to groan and complain about their pay. The landowner asks, "Didn't you agree to work for me for one day's wage?" They agree, but then they want to know why the guys that worked only one hour got the same pay. The first-hour workers were offended at the goodness of the landowner. His graciousness offended their sense of justice.

God's grace can have that impact on us, until we need that graciousness in our direction.

God eventually gives Jonah a personal lesson on grace, but we will look at that a little later. First let's look at the mindset that rejects God's graciousness.

CHAPTER 3

THE RELIGIOUS MINDSET

I CAN REMEMBER when I was a little kid in the summer; there were a few kids in our neighborhood that were around the same age. The world was a bit of a different place and we spent much of our time playing outside and only coming in to eat and to sleep. Summer days were long, spent riding bikes and exploring the world around us. One particular summer, for whatever reason, we were all obsessed with finding a four-leaf clover.

We all spent hours searching diligently through the grass to find this pseudomagical prize. We could never seem to find one until my next-door neighbor's older brother caught wind of our clover craze. Suddenly one afternoon he was finding them left and right. He was more than a little prideful of his ability to do so. There was a lot of gloating going on, to say the least.

I eventually through bartering and begging managed to get one of his many prized four-leaf clovers. I brought it into my house and quickly tucked it away in my *Encyclopedia Britannica*. Over dinner that night I proudly pulled it out to show my momma. She said, "Here, let me see that." I proudly handed it over to her and she took a closer look at it and said, "This isn't a real four-leaf clover." She began to show me where my neighbor's older brother had split one of the leaves and rounded the edges. I was so disappointed, because what I thought was the real thing was nothing more than a counterfeit.

There has always been a counterfeit. Jesus spent much of his earthly ministry calling out the counterfeit and revealing the real thing. If you'll notice, Jesus' harshest words were not toward the sinners, but toward the Pharisees and the Sadducees. He openly and consistently rebuked the religious leaders of the day. Let's look at just one of Jesus' many glorious statements in Matthew 23:27:

"Woe to you, scribes and Pharisees, hypocrites! For you are like whitewashed tombs which indeed appear beautiful outwardly, but inside are full of dead men's bones and all uncleanness."

Jesus is calling out the counterfeit, much like the four-leaf clovers being peddled by my neighbor's older brother: the Pharisees and Sadducees looked good from afar but closer inspection revealed that they were fakes. They were operating in a false godliness that looked good outwardly but inwardly was filled with death. This is what I like to refer to as "man-made religion." It is a very man-centered attempt to facilitate relationship with God, fueled mostly by the praise of man. This whole system is diametrically opposed to a true relationship with God that comes from the heart.

Nothing is more beautiful than a relationship with God; few things are as hideous as man-made religion; it promises a lot but only delivers death. It is this type of mindset that has given birth to some of the greatest atrocities in human history. Self-righteous religious hypocrisy has always been the greatest hurdle for what God is presently doing in the earth, because it masquerades around like it represents God. However, in actuality, it's just as fake as those four-leaf clovers.

How does all of this apply to what we are saying about Jonah, you may ask? Well, Jonah is a true man of God, called by God, with a message from God. I would assume in the beginning of Jonah's life and ministry he had a passion and excitement for serving God. I know how I was when I first received the call of God on my life. It was the most powerful thing that had ever happened to me. I was overwhelmed with the opportunity to represent God, the creator of all things, in the earth. What an absolute honor!

I can imagine that Jonah felt much the same way. However, his heart to serve God and represent him in the earth had changed. His own agenda had begun to be more important than representing God accurately. So much so that when God wanted him to share a message that was contrary to his agenda, he refused and even chose death over doing what God wanted. Jonah became man-centered instead of God-centered and chose to hold back the goodness of God because it didn't line up with his sense of justice.

Man-made religion is a disease and if not treated properly always leads to death. It may or may not be physical death but it will always bring death in some form. It may be death to a ministry, death to a relationship, death to the desire to serve God, death to relationship with God. When Jesus said it was filled with death, he wasn't kidding or mincing words. He was very serious and a good portion of his ministry was revealing this hypocrisy.

In these next few chapters we are going to look at the religious mindset in the lives of a few other people in the Bible. This will help us understand what

is going on in Jonah and ultimately help us understand what is going on in the modern-day Jonah's
who reject the message of amazing grace.

A TALE OF TWO SAULS

THE SAME RELIGIOUS mindset that afflicted Jonah afflicted the Pharisees and Sadducees, and it afflicts many people today. Keep in mind, none of us are exempt from this mindset. I spent a great many years under its heavy blinding yoke and I daresay that it's possible that there are still elements of it in my life. I don't say that to throw myself under the bus or freak you out to the point you set this book down and run away, but the reality is, no man holds all truth; we are all still learning in this life and not of us have "arrived."

The religious mindset happens in two primary ways. The first is, you just simply believe a lie and believing the lie causes you to reject the truth. That lie becomes a veil that darkens our eyes and dims our perception, so that when the truth is standing in front of us, we will still declare that it is a lie. For example, many of the Pharisees and Sadducees genuinely believed Jesus was a lunatic and not the son of God. Hey, even Jesus' family spent a portion of time thinking he was crazy and "beside himself." They eventually changed that view but for a time even they were blinded.

The Pharisees and Sadducees saw his graciousness and liberty and it didn't line up with what they knew about God. So what they already knew about God was blinding them to the most beautiful revelation of God that was standing right in front of them. Ironically their thoughts about God kept them from seeing God. That religious mindset blinded them to the point that they sought to kill God. So the first way it forms is simple ignorance; this is a much easier bout to cure.

The second is a little different, it is a willful rejection of truth because that truth doesn't line up with the best interests of our own personal agenda. Many of the people dealt with this brand of man-made religion as well. For example, in John 12:42-43 it says,

Nevertheless even among the rulers many believed in Him, but because of the Pharisees they did not confess Him, lest they should be put out of the synagogue; for they loved the praise of men more than the praise of God.

These people believed the truth that Jesus was the Christ but they loved the praise of men more than the praise of God. This brand of man-made religion is a little more resistant of a strain, because deliverance from the veil of the religious mindset happens when we embrace truth and recognize we were wrong. This requires humility and a desire to please God above pleasing man. Pride has a hard time admitting that it is wrong and pride is the hallmark of man-made religion.

In our study of the religious mindset, we will be looking at two different "Sauls." Both were afflicted by a religious mindset, both horribly persecuted people that had a real relationship with God. However, there are distinct differences between the two as well. One happened before the cross and one happened after the cross. One willfully rejected the truth and one simply did it in ignorance. One died with the disease of man-made religion and one was cured and went on to become one of the greatest ministers this world has ever seen. Both had a religious mindset that blinded them to the truth.

KING SAUL

HAVE YOU EVER seen anyone start out really good but end up really bad? It can be very tragic. I can remember a guy I used to go to school with; he was a very gifted athlete. He almost looked like a grown man even in grade school. He was stronger and faster than anyone we knew. Athletically, everything he set his hand to prospered—he was just amazingly gifted. His primary sport was boxing and his coach was grooming him to be a Golden Gloves winner and then hopefully to go onto the Olympics.

I moved and finished out school in another part of the state. I just assumed that one day I would hear this guy's name again because he seemed to be destined for fame. Years later I saw his sister out and asked how he was doing. She told me that he fell into the wrong crowd as he got older and got involved with drugs. She said he died at twenty-two years of age when he was killed in a drive-by shooting. I was so sorry to hear that and tried to comfort her the best I could.

I was truly surprised because to look at the beginning of his life all the pieces were lined up for greatness. I thought for sure he would have ended up famous and successful, but even though God love him, he squandered it and died tragically. The gentleman we are about to talk about had a similar path. He began his life with every indicator of greatness but his life ended tragically as well. He became a casualty of man-made religion but we can learn some things from the mistakes in his life that will help us in ours.

Few accounts in the Bible more clearly display the difference between relationship and man-made religion than King Saul and David. David, the man after God's own heart, had a dynamic relationship with God that transcended all his earthly experiences. Saul began well but lost his way. Saul eventually gravitated toward a man-pleasing external religious performance before the people rather than a heart-based relationship with God. Saul was an honorable and good man; he just lost his way and sold out to man-made religions attractive deception. The enemy is very subtle in his lies, and King Saul took the bait.

1 Samuel 9:27- 10:

As they were going down to the outskirts of the city, Samuel said to Saul, "Tell the servant to go on ahead of us." And he went on, "But you stand here a while, that I may announce to you the word of God." Then Samuel took a flask of oil and poured it on his head, and kissed him and said: "Is it not because the Lord has anointed you commander over His inheritance?"

Who anointed him commander? God did. God chose Saul, God anointed Saul, God gifted and empowered Saul to fulfill a powerful and ground-breaking calling. Saul would be the first king of Israel. No one had ever done anything like this before. Saul was special and Saul was chosen.

Saul then goes on from this experience of being anointed as king at the hands of the prophet Samuel to have a supernatural encounter with God. He meets a company of prophets and the Lord causes him to prophesy and gives him a new heart. Powerful stuff, right? So Saul, with a heart after God, begins to fulfill his calling. He unifies the children of Israel into a kingdom. Saul fights the Lord's battles and begins to bring a sense of strength and oneness to God's people.

Saul truly begins beautifully, but along the way his own agenda tragically begins to supersede the will of God in his life. Slowly that deceptive veil of man-centered religion begins to form and blinds his eyes to the truth. Slowly pride and self-exaltation begin to arise and it's no longer about God or even about God's people. Slowly it becomes all about Saul and his agenda and his best interest. It ends up destroying his life and bringing great destruction to the lives of those around him. Let's fast-forward a bit in the story of his life and look at the outward manifestation of what was already present in his heart. Here it appears Saul commits a seemingly small act of disobedience, at least in comparison to the things King David would eventually do after him, but we have to remember that the Lord looks at the heart, not just the action. That religious mindset that was forming in Saul was very dangerous. After a battle Saul doesn't follow through with the Lord's orders to destroy the Amalekites. He spares the king and keeps the goods and livestock for himself and the people.

1 Samuel 15:10–12

Now the word of the Lord came to Samuel, saying, "I greatly regret that I have set up Saul as king, for he has turned back from following Me,

and has not performed My commandments."
And it grieved Samuel, and he cried out to the
Lord all night.

So, when Samuel rose early in the morning
to meet Saul, it was told Samuel, saying,
"Saul went to Carmel, and indeed, he set up
a monument for himself; and he has gone on
around, passed by, and gone down to Gilgal."

Notice after the victory Saul immediately sets up a monument FOR HIMSELF. The infiltration of man-made religion always exalts and even deifies self. Saul doesn't celebrate the Lord, giving him the victory in the battle. Saul celebrates himself and his own strength. He wants everyone to remember just how awesome he is. I always jokingly say the song of man-made religion is "How great I am" instead of "How great thou art." Saul is getting caught up in himself and this mindset of man-made religion is already beginning to cloud his judgement. We continue in the next verse.

Then Samuel went to Saul, and Saul said to him, "Blessed are you of the Lord! I have performed the commandment of the Lord."

But Samuel said, "What then is this bleating

of the sheep in my ears, and the lowing of the oxen which I hear?"

Notice, Saul begins with all the cool religious things to say, "Blessed are you of the Lord! I have performed the commandment of the Lord." His heart is not toward the Lord at all but he knows that right religious things to say. Saul has already slipped over into performing. Samuel immediately calls him out and says hey if you have obeyed the Lord, why do I hear sheep and oxen? We then see Saul's response in the next verse.

And Saul said, "They have brought them from the Amalekites; for the people spared the best of the sheep and the oxen, to sacrifice to the Lord your God; and the rest we have utterly destroyed."

First, he blames the people (man-made religion specializes in accusation and blame shifting), then he tries to cover his tracks by once again throwing some religious performance in the mix by talking about making sacrifices "unto the Lord." Of course, Samuel is having none of it and immediately calls him out again in the next verse. (Samuel has a real relationship with God, not a religious performance before the people.)

Then Samuel said to Saul, "Be quiet! And I will tell you what the Lord said to me last night."

And he said to him, "Speak on."

So Samuel said, "When you were little in your own eyes, were you not head of the tribes of Israel? And did not the Lord anoint you king over Israel? Now the Lord sent you on a mission, and said, 'Go, and utterly destroy the sinners, the Amalekites, and fight against them until they are consumed.' Why then did you not obey the voice of the Lord? Why did you swoop down on the spoil, and do evil in the sight of the Lord?"

Saul then tries to justify himself in the next verse.

And Saul said to Samuel, "But I have obeyed the voice of the Lord, and gone on the mission on which the Lord sent me, and brought back Agag king of Amalek; I have utterly destroyed the Amalekites. But the people took of the plunder, sheep and oxen, the best of the things which should have been utterly destroyed, to sacrifice to the Lord your God in Gilgal."

I want to bring a very important point out here: man-made religion is always more concerned with what people think than what God thinks. Saul says the people made him do it and then he tries to cover his rebellion against God with religious acts of worship in the form of sacrifices. Then in the next verse Samuel addresses the very heart of the matter.

So Samuel said:

*"Has the Lord as great delight in burnt offerings
and sacrifices,*

As in obeying the voice of the Lord?
Behold, to obey is better than sacrifice,
And to heed than the fat of rams.
For rebellion is as the sin of witchcraft,
And stubbornness is as iniquity and idolatry.
Because you have rejected the word of the Lord,
He also has rejected you from being king."

Samuel basically says in this statement, your display of so-called devotion with these intended sacrifices are just a cover-up for your stubborn rebellious heart. Saul stubbornly elevated his own plans above God's plan. Then he tried to cover it up with religious words and actions of devotion that were not in any way in his heart. This ultimately leads to hero worship and idolatry—that's why we see Saul erect a monument to himself. Man-made religion always leads to worship of man and not God. Now, as Saul is confronted with the truth, he has an opportunity to allow this veil to be removed. He has an opportunity to forsake this religious mindset and be cured, but instead of humbling himself and receiving correction, he hunkers down in his rebellion and chooses the "religious show" before the people, rather than having a heart relationship with God. Then as the whole scenario begins to play out in the next few verses, we see the true motivation of Saul's heart.

Then Saul said to Samuel, "I have sinned, for I have transgressed the commandment of the Lord and your words, because I feared the people and obeyed their voice. Now therefore, please pardon my sin, and return with me, that I may worship the Lord."

For a moment it seems as though Saul is ready to repent and live from his heart in relationship with the Lord rather than a wear the religious mask, but Samuel, being a prophet, discerns his true motives. We then see his true motivation revealed in the next few verses.

But Samuel said to Saul, "I will not return with you, for you have rejected the word of the Lord, and the Lord has rejected you from being king over Israel."

And as Samuel turned around to go away, Saul seized the edge of his robe, and it tore. So Samuel said to him, "The Lord has torn the kingdom of Israel from you today, and has given it to a neighbor of yours, who is better than you. And also the Strength of Israel will not lie nor relent. For He is not a man, that He should relent."

Then he said, "I have sinned; yet honor me now,

please, before the elders of my people and before Israel, and return with me, that I may worship the Lord your God." So Samuel turned back after Saul, and Saul worshipped the Lord.

Saul desperately begs Samuel to have a worship service with him, not because he wants to turn his heart to the Lord but because he wants to look good in front of the people. Samuel humors him and turns to worship with him before the people. Then, ladies and gentlemen, we have possibly the very first religious church worship service. Saul is not truly worshipping God here; Saul is religiously performing before the people for their honor and admiration. The only worshipping going on here is Saul worshipping himself as he basks in the admiration of the people.

From this time forward Saul would grow worse and worse and increasingly more desperate. So much so that when a young man would enter in on the scene who did have a relationship with God, Saul's heart would be consumed with murdering that young man. David was a man whose life was clearly filled with failures and faults but David never got caught up in performing for the people. David lived his life as unto the Lord, in relationship with him.

Let's look at the end of King Saul's life. He chooses to reject truth and the religious mindset, and he begins to destroy his life and the lives of those around him. He grows increasingly more prideful as his focus is off God and unto himself. He also continues to grow increasingly more paranoid at the thought of losing his control and power. These poisonous forces in his heart culminate in a deep hatred for David, a man who does not have a religious mindset but has a genuine relationship with God. We pick it up in scripture on the very last day of Saul's life in 1 Samuel 31:1:

Now the Philistines fought against Israel; and the men of Israel fled from before the Philistines, and fell slain on Mount Gilboa. Then the Philistines followed hard after Saul and his sons. And the Philistines killed Jonathan, Abinadab, and Malchishua, Saul's sons. The battle became fierce against Saul. The archers hit him, and he was severely wounded by the archers.

Then Saul said to his armor-bearer, "Draw your sword, and thrust me through with it, lest these uncircumcised men come and thrust me through and abuse me."

But his armor-bearer would not, for he was greatly afraid. Therefore Saul took a sword and fell on it. And when his armor-bearer saw that Saul was dead, he also fell on his sword, and died with him.

Saul is so full of pride he takes his own life rather than having an enemy do it. That religious spirit is a destroyer and it leads down a very destructive path. It is a horrible evil and the enemy does his greatest damage through it. We see King Saul at the end of his tragic life never reaching a place of repentance and change. The wonderful calling that God had for his life was unfulfilled and as the sun set on his life the only one rejoicing was the enemy. Now, I know this is a very dramatic scenario. I'm not saying everyone with a religious mindset is going to meet the same end as King Saul, but I am saying that this mindset is very destructive and can do a great deal of damage.

Now I want to stop and say, don't think I'm being too hard on Saul—I just want to expose the disease of man-made religion that took over his heart. Understanding this will help us to understand what is going on in the hearts of the modern-day ministers that reject the message of grace.

In the next chapter we will take a look at another Saul, Saul of Tarsus, who eventually becomes the apostle Paul. We will discuss their similarities and contrast their differences. Both show us what happens to a life when it is blinded by a religious mindset.

CHAPTER 6

SAUL BECOMES PAUL

Now, LET'S TAKE a look at another Saul, who began his life blinded by a religious mindset but was set free from it as he embraced truth. One of the major differences between the two Sauls is one happened before the cross and one happened after the cross. One Saul gets set free and goes onto become a great man of God; the other Saul dies on the battlefield of his own selfishness.

The redemption power of God in many ways was limited before Jesus came. For example, if someone was possessed with a demon in the old covenant the prescribed method of deliverance was to stone them. The demon couldn't yet be separated from the person and the method of healing for the community of people was to simply remove the person, kind of like throwing out a bad apple so the other apples don't go bad as well.

Many issues were handled like that under the old covenant, but then Jesus hits the scene and everything changes. A prostitute who has seven demons encounters Jesus and the demons are cast out and she becomes one of Jesus' most devout disciples. Jesus as savior greatly increases the redeeming power of God in the earth. So what was a life-destroying issue for King Saul is not for Saul of Tarsus. In fact, Saul gets delivered from a religious mindset to become one of the greatest apostles to ever live.

Now before we step into this next portion of teaching I want to say that I do not believe anything in the Bible is there by coincidence, including names. Names are filled with meaning and many times people and even places represent things. For example, the apostle Paul refers to Hagar to represent law as a system of bondage.

Galatians 4:22

For it is written that Abraham had two sons: the one by a bondwoman, the other by a freewoman. But he who was of the bondwoman was born according to the flesh, and he of the freewoman through promise, which things are symbolic. For these are the two covenants: the one from Mount Sinai which gives birth to bondage, which is Hagar.

Paul uses these Old Testament characters symbolically to convey the difference between law and grace. He takes a passage of the Old Testament and, by the spirit, filters it through the cross to reveal Jesus and his amazing grace. Just another quick example of this would be in 2 Samuel 9, King David searches for Mephibosheth to bless him and finds him in a land called Lo Debar. Lo Debar means a place that has no pasture, a place of poverty, lack, and not enough. David brings him out of Lo Debar and brings Mephibosheth to the king's table to enjoy an inheritance. No detail is put in scripture by accident; the Holy Spirit is purposely adding these things to teach us if we will take the time to study it out.

The name Saul, comes to represent a person dominated by a religious mindset. The first Saul dies with it, and the second Saul gets delivered from the religious mindset and drops the name Saul to become the apostle Paul.

Paul goes on to have a mighty ministry and is chosen to reveal the message of amazing grace to the gentile world. I like to say every Saul is one donkey slip away from becoming a Paul.

Both men meant well, but both men ended up attacking the very things God was doing in the earth; the only difference is one received redemption and one ended up in destruction. We will look later at why one changed and why one stayed the same but for now let's look at Saul of Tarsus.

The first mention we find of Saul of Tarsus is in the book of Acts. We find him actively persecuting the church. We pick it up in Acts 7:58–8:1:

> and they cast him out of the city and stoned him. And the witnesses laid down their clothes at the feet of a young man named Saul. And they stoned Stephen as he was calling on God and saying, "Lord Jesus, receive my spirit." Then he knelt down and cried out with a loud voice, "Lord, do not charge them with this sin." And when he had said this, he fell asleep. Now Saul was consenting to his death.

Here is Saul operating in a religious mindset attacking the present move of God in the earth. Man-made religion always attacks what God is presently doing and many times they do it unaware that they are defying God's will. Quite often they are simply doing it in ignorance, because they are operating in what they have always known rather than operating out of a right now relationship with

God. When Saul of Tarsus is doing these things, he thinks he is working with God to stamp out these blasphemous Jesus believers. We pick it up in the next verses:

And there arose on that day a great persecution against the church which was in Jerusalem; and they were all scattered abroad throughout the regions of Judaea and Samaria, except the apostles. And devout men buried Stephen, and made great lamentation over him. But Saul laid waste the church, entering into every house, and dragging men and women committed them to prison. They therefore that were scattered abroad, went about preaching the word.

Saul, representing the religious mindset, is laying waste to the early church, persecuting with all his might, the present move of God—that is, until he encounters Jesus. The difference between King Saul and this Saul is one happens before the cross and the other happens after the cross. King Saul died a lonely death on a hill during a raging battle. Saul of Tarsus encountered Jesus on the road to Damascus and became a new man. One encounter with Jesus will change your name, your identity, your heart, and your passion.

On the road to Damascus to persecute Christians, Saul became a Christian, when he encountered the King of Kings. Jesus took Saul's destructive zeal that was destroying the early church and turned it to build the early church.

One of the things I feel the Lord wants me to do in this book is give some perspective into the mindset of man-made religion, not only for exposing it, but also for the purpose of producing compassion for the people gripped in its lies. There is a powerful redemption for these leaders who are attacking the grace of God.

These leaders, no matter how much they attack and persecute you, are not the enemy. We do not war against flesh and blood. No human being on this planet has ever been or ever will be your enemy. We have an enemy, the devil, and one of his primary attacks is false teaching, trying to confuse us by mixing the old and new covenants together. Ephesians 6:12 says,

For our struggle is not against flesh and blood, but against the rulers, against the authorities, against the powers of this dark world and against the spiritual forces of evil in the heavenly realms.

It is important to remember our enemy isn't Saul. Our enemy is the spiritual force keeping Saul, and those like him, in bondage to religion and self-righteousness.

We have already stated that one of the main differences between King Saul and Saul of Tarsus is that one happened before the cross and one happened after the cross. Now, let's take a look at another very fundamental difference. We find it in Paul's own words in 1 Timothy 1:12–13,

And I thank Christ Jesus our Lord who has enabled me, because He counted me faithful, putting me into the ministry, although I was formerly a blasphemer, a persecutor, and an insolent man; but I obtained mercy because I did it ignorantly in unbelief.

Paul was consumed with a blinding religious mindset but it was a result of ignorance, not a stubborn, prideful, rejection of the truth. You can see his heart so clearly on the road to Damascus as he repents immediately as he encounters Jesus. We pick up the account in Acts 9:3–6.

As he journeyed he came near Damascus, and suddenly a light shone around him from heaven. Then he fell to the ground, and heard a voice saying to him, "Saul, Saul, why are you persecuting Me?"

And he said, "Who are You, Lord?"

Then the Lord said, "I am Jesus, whom you

are persecuting. It is hard for you to kick against the goads."

So he, trembling and astonished, said, "Lord, what do You want me to do?"

Saul's immediate response as he encounters the truth, is "What do you want me to do?" As soon as truth comes and Paul knows it's truth he is ready to drop this religious veil. Now, mind you, this was a very dramatic experience and not everyone is going to have an experience like this but people eventually have a choice to accept or reject truth. So we see that Paul's blindness is in part a result of his ignorance.

There are many leaders who attack grace today in the modern-day church simply because they do not know or they do not understand what the gospel of grace is really saying. I spent a portion of my life standing against the message of grace, mostly because I thought it was a message that told people it was OK to live a lifestyle of sin. So, in my ignorance I initially rejected the truth and, to be honest, it took me a while to embrace certain aspects of the message of grace.

I can remember as the gospel began to shine on my mind, that old religious mindset fought back against the truth. It started as I read the book *Destined to Reign* by Joseph Prince, which introduced me to the message of grace in a way I could understand. I frequently got mad and even threw the book across the room, yelling "Heresy!" Sometimes religious mindsets are a little painful to let go off as truth begins to cut through the veil of lies. When you've spent a portion of your life seeing something a certain way and standing on what you think is a foundation of truth, when that foundation gets rocked, it can be a very traumatic time.

Then, after I threw the book across the room, I would go back and pick it up again and open my Bible to see that the truths that were being presented were scriptural, just different than what I had been taught. It was a process, and I am in no way saying I have arrived. I am still learning, as everyone is. However, what I did find happening to me as my heart began to be established in grace was that the most beautiful fruit began to start growing on my branches. Fruit that I longed for and even pretended that I had under legalism but now this fruit was real fruit, based on Jesus' strength and not my own. Slowly I began to realize that this "too good to be true" news was actually really the gospel of Jesus Christ. I then began to preach the message I used to attack.

As you are reading this book you may be on the fence about the gospel of grace or you may have a Saul in your life right now. A leader who doesn't understand the gospel and is actively persecuting the message. I encourage you to pray for them. No one!—I repeat, no one!— is too far gone for Jesus! I used to attack this message and now I've written three books about it.

Don't demonize this person and seek their destruction, don't fall into the slander game of he said, she said. Stay above all of that and, like David did, don't raise your hand against this child of God who has lost their way. Instead pray for them! Pray that they have an encounter with Jesus and slip off that donkey to become a person that carries the heart of God, not the heavy persecuting hand of religion.

JONAH'S PERSONAL LESSON ON GRACE

We HAVE BEEN looking at the impact of the religious mindset on leaders. Two different Sauls with two totally different results. Understanding this mindset will help us understand why many different modern-day leaders reject and refuse to preach the liberating message of grace. As we have seen, some folks do it out of ignorance and some willfully reject the truth.

As you may remember, we began this journey studying the life of Jonah. Let's get back to our friend Jonah and draw some more truths from his life concerning this, but first let me share a little truth with you about how God operates. We have already talked a little about this concept in reference to King Saul and Saul of Tarsus but I want to reiterate this point again briefly.

In Proverbs 25:2 it says:

It is the glory of God to conceal a matter,

But the glory of kings is to search out a matter.

I have an eleven-year-old son and when he was little my wife and I used to love to play this game with him we called warmer or colder. We would hide something from him like candy or a toy or something and then he would search for it. When he got closer we would say warmer and we he got further away from it we would say colder and until eventually he would find it and be thrilled by his prize. Now, we didn't hide it from him so he couldn't find it; we hid it for him so he could find it and have the joy of discovering where it was. God does the exact same thing for us in many different ways—remember he is a loving Father.

God loves to hide things in his word for us to discover. I sometimes feel like it is a big puzzle that I have been working on for most of my life. Periodically I get another piece to help me understand who he is and what his plan is in my life. I love it! It's exciting! What I'm honored to share with you next is another piece of the puzzle.

There is a detail in the account of Jonah that we

could simply look over without thinking it had any significance. Let's look at the account again.

Jonah 1:1–3

Now the word of Jehovah came unto Jonah the son of Amittai, saying, Arise, go to Nineveh, that great city, and cry against it; for their wickedness is come up before me. But Jonah rose up to flee unto Tarshish from the presence of Jehovah; and he went down to Joppa, and found a ship going to Tarshish: so he paid the fare thereof, and went down into it, to go with them unto Tarshish from the presence of Jehovah.

We know Jonah is trying to run from the presence of God because he doesn't want to preach the message that God is calling him to preach, but where is Jonah running to? A land called Tarshish, and just to be sure we don't miss this detail, God says it three times in the same sentence. So where in the world is Tarshish? Many scholars agree and more specifically the well-respected first century A.D. Jewish historian Flavius Josephus wrote that it was the same city as Tarsus in modern day Turkey, which the apostle Paul's hometown.

Jonah was running away from the presence of God to what would eventually be Saul's hometown!

What I believe God is trying to show us here through the scriptures is that Jonah is dealing with this same religious spirit that King Saul and the apostle Paul dealt with. The enemy does not have any new tricks; he just uses the same tricks repeatedly. That religious mindset was once again trying to block what God wanted to do in the earth. God had a plan to save the people of Nineveh but Jonah was exalting his own ideas and plans above God's.

As we have begun to understand the religious mindset we can begin to understand why a man of God would reject a message from God and desire to destroy what God desires to save.

God is about give Jonah a personal lesson on grace. When Jonah finally repents after the whole, in the belly of the whale scenario, he goes to Ninevah and begins to preach this message that he had received from the Lord. To his disappointment, the people begin to repent and change their ways and are saved from the all the consequences of their actions.

Jonah should be excited, right? The people are saved and receive mercy rather than judgement. Jonah is not excited at all; in fact he is angry with God for being merciful to these wicked sinners and not giving them what they "deserve." We pick up the story in Jonah 3:1–6:

Now the word of the Lord came to Jonah the second time, saying, "Arise, go to Nineveh, that great city, and preach to it the message that I tell you." So Jonah arose and went to Nineveh, according to the word of the Lord. Now Nineveh was an exceedingly great city, a three-day journey in extent. And Jonah began to enter the city on the first day's walk. Then he cried out and said, "Yet forty days, and Nineveh shall be overthrown!"

So the people of Nineveh believed God, proclaimed a fast, and put on sackcloth, from the greatest to the least of them.

The people believed his message from God. This was a message of God's goodness and his desire to save these people from the dire consequences of their actions.

Jonah 3:10:

Then God saw their works, that they turned from their evil way; and God relented from the disaster that He had said He would bring upon them, and He did not do it.

The Bible says God delights in mercy, not Judgement. God is delighted that these people of have turned from their wicked ways and the mercy of God can now overshadow their failures. God has a plan of hope and redemption for their future. All of heaven is rejoicing! Unfortunately, the preacher is not rejoicing in this lavish display of mercy. The preacher wanted judgement, not mercy. We pick up the story in the next chapter:

Jonah 4:1–2

But it displeased Jonah exceedingly, and he became angry. So he prayed to the Lord, and said, "Ah, Lord, was not this what I said when I was still in my country? Therefore I fled previously to Tarshish; for I know that You are a gracious and merciful God, slow to anger and abundant in loving-kindness, One who relents from doing harm."

Jonah knows God is good! Jonah knows God is gracious! Jonah knows God is merciful and slow to anger and abundant in loving-kindness! But, Jonah wanted God to bring judgement and destruction on these people, not mercy, grace, and kindness. Then Jonah makes the most astonishing statement in the next verse.

Jonah 4:3

"Therefore now, O Lord, please take my life from me, for it is better for me to die than to live!"

Jonah wants to die; he sounds almost like a child throwing a temper tantrum. "If I can't get my way and bring judgement on these people, I'll just lay down and die." Then God begins to try and minister to him through his stubbornness.

Jonah 4:4

Then the Lord said, "Is it right for you to be angry?"

Jonah doesn't even answer God; he just walks out of the city and sits on a hill to see what God is going to do. God still loves and wants to reach his angry preacher, so he prepares some circumstances to try and reach Jonah's angry heart.

Jonah 4:5

So Jonah went out of the city and sat on the east side of the city. There he made himself a shelter and sat under it in the shade, till he might see what would become of the city. And the Lord God prepared a plant and made it come up over Jonah, that it might be shade for his head to deliver him from his misery. So, Jonah was very grateful for the plant.

God shows Jonah mercy even during his rebellion and stubbornness. Jonah was angry and in rebellion about God's mercy and graciousness. God creates a plant to provide shade and refreshment for Jonah as he sits on the hill angrily watching the city.

Jonah 4:7

But as morning dawned the next day God prepared a worm, and it so damaged the plant that it withered. And it happened, when the sun arose, that God prepared a vehement east wind; and the sun beat on Jonah's head, so that he grew faint. Then he wished death for himself, and said, "It is better for me to die than to live."

Then God removes the shade of the plant and asks Jonah a question to help him see the error of heart.

Jonah 4:9

Then God said to Jonah, "Is it right for you to be angry about the plant?"

And he said, "It is right for me to be angry, even to death!"

Yes, Jonah is still mad about all this mercy and grace but then God asks him another question.

Jonah 4:10

But the Lord said, "You have had pity on the plant for which you have not labored, nor made it grow, which came up in a night and perished in a night. And should I not pity Nineveh, that great city, in which are more than one hundred and twenty thousand persons who cannot discern between their right hand and their left—and much livestock?"

The key here is this statement God makes about the plant: "You have not labored, nor made it grow." God is trying to reveal grace to this angry preacher. You did nothing to deserve this protection that I just sent you. In fact now Jonah is in absolute rebellion against God. The sailors on the ship he was trying to use to escape on were more receptive to God than Jonah was.

It's truly amazing how that religious mindset can blind us. Yet God is graciously showing him mercy. Then, when the plant that is giving him cover dies, Jonah gets really upset. God said you have had more pity for this plant than an entire city of people that don't know the difference between right and wrong. This exchange reveals another aspect of the religious mindset: folks want mercy for themselves but not for others.

This reminds me of one of the parables Jesus uses

to explain the kingdom of God. A servant owes the king a massive amount of money. The king mercifully forgives the debt, but afterward the servant goes out finds someone that owes him a small amount of money and takes him by the throat and throws him into prison until he can pay it all. God is addressing this attitude in Jonah's heart and gives him a personal lesson in grace. Right after this lesson on grace the book ends and we never find out if Jonah receives the correction or not.

CHAPTER 8

A RETURN TO GRACE

WE ARE CURRENTLY experiencing the most beautiful reformation in the body of Christ. People everywhere across our nation and all over the world are returning to Jesus and his amazing grace. The simple, powerful message of the gospel is being restored as the solid foundation that we build on. Man-made religion's weak foundation of dead works is being removed and replaced. The powerful cornerstone of Jesus and his righteousness is being restored to the body of Christ. Reformation is not always a nice, neat, easy process. The whole thing reminds me of the passage in Jeremiah 1:9-10:

Then the Lord put forth His hand and touched my mouth, and the Lord said to me:

"Behold, I have put My words in your mouth.

See, I have this day set you over the nations and over the kingdoms,

To root out and to pull down,

To destroy and to throw down,

To build and to plant."

I can remember, early in our ministry, my wife and I took over a youth group that had been turned into a teen center. When we walked into the sanctuary, the platform was so high that it absolutely towered over the kids. The pulpit was perched on top of this skyscraper-like stage, like a towering, intimidating judgement seat. It seemed very cold, condescending, and distant. When we took over, there was just a handful of kids there and they seemed swallowed up and minimized by that cold sanctuary. The kids were so far away from the minister it was like they were just little peons looking up at the judge's gavel. My wife and I knew it was time for some reformation. We immediately tore down that big intimidating platform and began to renovate that entire youth ministry. Reformation is messy but it's necessary for change. There was a lot of rooting out, pulling down, and throwing down before we could build and plant, but after we were done that youth ministry began to thrive and it became a warm inviting place.

I know when I began to hear the gospel it rocked

me to my core as I realized the foundation of my belief system wasn't Jesus and his finished work on the cross. Yes, I got saved by grace but I quickly departed from it and walked down the road of legalism to establish my own righteousness and attempt to earn God's favor and blessing. My foundation had been tampered with by doctrines that exalted man and his efforts instead of exalting Jesus and his finished work. The results were not good to say the least; the joy that I began my Christianity with was gone.

The confidence I had in my forgiveness before God had evaporated and I lived in a miserable existence of insecurity not knowing if God was mad at me or pleased with me. That heavy yoke of legalism had begun to crush the life out of me. But Jesus! He came dashing in to save me from the horrors of man-made religion with his amazing grace.

Grace came in like a warm flood of love and began to sweep away all the bricks of fear and condemnation that had been built in my mind. God by the power of his gospel was pulling down the strongholds that had been built in my mind. In many ways it was a very challenging and scary process as the false things I trusted in and had built my confidence on were being removed. The warm steady flow of love that the gospel brings washed through my belief system like a pressure washer, bringing me all the way down to my foundation. Then my broken foundation was removed and replaced with the strong cornerstone of Jesus and his finished work on the cross. Then God began to put the good truths that I had learned back into place on this solid foundation. The whole process reminds me of the apostle Paul talking about being a wise master builder in 1 Corinthians 3:10:

According to the grace of God which was given to me, as a wise master builder I have laid the foundation, and another builds on it. But let each one take heed how he builds on it.

My foundation was off as a result of man-centered teaching and when your foundation is off, everything that you build on it will be off also. My life and ministry were being radically changed. It was a simple, beautiful return to grace but there was a huge dynamic reformation that took place inside of me. The whole thing reminds me of the words of Jesus in Matthew 11:28 (paraphrased):

"Are you tired? Worn out? Burned out on religion? Come to me. Get away with me and you'll recover your life. I'll show you how to take a real rest. Walk with me and work with me—watch how I do it. Learn the unforced rhythms of grace. I won't lay anything heavy or ill-fitting on you. Keep company with me and you'll learn to live freely and lightly."

People are burned out with man-made religion and their hearts are longing for Jesus, even when they don't know it. They just know things aren't working and something must be wrong but many times they can't quite put their finger on it. I see people in my own church and across this nation as I travel and minister who feel like a part of their life has been stolen from them by man-made religion. Jesus is tossing the temple tables and setting the captives free. A great reformation is upon us!

When I heard the gospel of grace again for the first time in a long time, it was like I had been holding my breath for fourteen years and finally got to breathe again. I began to fill my lungs with huge gulps of amazing grace. Life returned to me, life returned to my marriage, life returned to my family and my ministry. I became alive with the love of God as I was reminded how much God truly loved me. I was serving as an associate pastor at the church I was at, at the time. I was so excited and began to immediately preach this message that brought so much life to me and my family. Initially, everyone was excited and the people gladly received the message. We ordered new grace-based books for our bookstore. People became genuinely enthusiastic and joyful.

It was a very exciting time because it was as if we were all being reintroduced to Jesus. I remember hearing many people say, "It feels like I have been born again, again." Of course, they weren't—you only get born again one time—but they were experiencing amazing grace all over again just like I had. People's hearts were being filled with love as they were returning to their first love, Jesus.

It was a pretty awesome time in the beginning. However, there was a group of people who were becoming less and less excited about what was going on, specifically, the top leadership of the church. You see, when you preach the true gospel and bring the focus back to Jesus, there are some things that begin to change. One of the defining elements of Jesus' presence is freedom, not control. As the gospel is preached it begins to take the focus off of man and bring it back onto Jesus and an atmosphere of liberty is created.

You can't preach this gospel and control people at the same time. You can't preach this gospel and take all the credit anymore. You can't preach this gospel and force people to give or scare people into attending church anymore. The gospel always brings freedom. Where the spirit of the Lord is, there will be liberty. The tools of control are removed from the hands of the ministers and they must trust God and his spirit to bring forth fruit. No more controlling people through guilt, condemnation, and fear. So many of the tools that were used to build this ministry slowly began to be taken away as Jesus was glorified and lifted up through his amazing grace.

When the bricks in your building are guilt, condemnation, and fear the entire structure begins to dissolve when those motivations are removed. Now God did not desire to destroy this ministry in any way but the wood, hay, and stubble was being burnt up so the foundation could be reset. The same beautiful reformation that had happened inside of me was beginning to happen in this church. The people were gladly receiving it but the leadership began to reject it. The dynamics of a ministry begins to change when Jesus is the cornerstone and central focus; it's a wonderful thing but it can be a scary thing for leaders who have trusted in things other than Jesus to build their ministry.

Without Jesus as the cornerstone and the central focus, everything that is built only glorifies man and man's efforts.

God is not looking to glorify pastors or denominations or nondenominations. God is looking to glorify his son. When Jesus is glorified, everyone is edified; when man is glorified, people are brought low and it creates and unhealthy environment where one group of people are exalted above another, and then a fear-filled control is right around the corner.

Needless to say, the leaders began to take notice and they didn't like losing control, as the atmosphere of Jesus and his liberty where beginning to develop. Now, I don't want to paint them out as bad people, any more than I want to paint King Saul, the apostle Paul, or Jonah as a bad person. That veil of religion had slowly grown over their hearts and blinded them to Jesus and what he was doing at that moment. (We all must guard against this because it can happen to any of us.)

They slowly and unknowingly began to exchange Jesus and his amazing grace for the tools of legalism. Guilt, fear, condemnation, and control can bring a quicker change in people's behavior, but they have no ability to transform people's lives and touch their hearts. They have no ability to cause people to fall in love with their savior—only amazing grace can do that.

It can be easy to turn to Hagar to produce, rather

than wait on Sarah, but Sarah brings forth Isaacs, while Hagar can only bring forth Ishmaels.

Grace takes longer but it brings forth genuine fruit that is based on God's strength and not our own. Only amazing grace can bring forth the promise.

As I'm sharing these experiences from my own life, I hope it helps you to understand and maybe even relate to the much-needed reformation that is sweeping across the world.

As I have traveled across this nation preaching the gospel, I have found that my experience is not isolated or uncommon. I regularly meet people who are so wounded by the abuse of man-made religion it's absolutely horrifying. I have just wept as I have heard what has been done to people. Many of them walk away from the church, and some of them try to walk away from God.

It was the exact same way in Jesus' day. The people readily received him and the message that he preached, but the leaders struggled to receive him because they were more interested in power, glory, and control. As it was then so it is now.

Eventually all the grace-based books were pulled from the bookstore and the message was openly attacked from the pulpit. Truly a sad day for that church and ministry. I stayed there for another year but I began to depart internally as I became more alive to Jesus and his amazing grace. To this day, I am praying that this ministry will be restored to a healthy place of grace.

HOW TO HANDLE THE LEADERS WHO ATTACK THE GOSPEL

So how do we handle these leaders who refuse to preach the gospel and even attack it? When the leader is not directly involved in your life, it's quite easy to handle them. Just pray for them and move on with your own life. However, it's a little more challenging when you are sitting under the leader or are working together with them in ministry. Now each situation is different, so it is real hard to present a blueprint here. What I think is more important than the how we handle this is the attitude we have during the situation.

I think we can glean a great deal of wisdom from the way David handled Saul. David, a man after God's own heart, with a real relationship with God, lived under the oppressive atmosphere created by King Saul, who had embraced a religious mindset. Saul was very jealous of David and had committed himself to destroying David any way he could. Saul's attacks against David began as lies and slander against David's character, but Saul's rage grew to the point that he was hunting David down daily to kill him.

Through a series of events David had an opportunity to kill Saul and end all his problems. Look at how David handles this as we pick up the account in 1 Samuel 24:2–9:

> *Then Saul took three thousand chosen men from all Israel, and went to seek David and his men on the Rocks of the Wild Goats. So he came to the sheepfolds by the road, where there was a cave; and Saul went in to attend to his needs. [David and his men were staying in the recesses of the cave.] Then the men of David said to him, "This is the day of which the Lord said to you, 'Behold, I will deliver your enemy into your hand, that you may do to him as it seems good to you.'" And David arose and secretly cut off a corner of Saul's robe. Now it happened afterward that David's heart troubled him because he had cut Saul's robe. And he said to his men, "The Lord forbid*

that I should do this thing to my master, the Lord's anointed, to stretch out my hand against him, seeing he is the anointed of the Lord." So David restrained his servants with these words and did not allow them to rise against Saul. And Saul got up from the cave and went on his way.

Now, there are some powerful truths in this passage of scripture on how to handle a leader who has given himself over to a religious mindset. I'll begin by saying hopefully in the modern-day church no one is even thinking about killing someone but we can kill someone with our words without lifting an actual sword.

One of the things we unfortunately deal with in our society is people assassinating someone else's character by slandering them. This happens way too often in the body of Christ, especially when there are doctrinal differences. I would like to say that slander should never be a tool in the Christian's toolbox. Slander and accusation is how the devil operates, not Christianity. So what does David do?

It looks as though Saul has been delivered into David's hands and some of David's men are even quoting prophecy to him trying to get him to kill Saul and remove this problem for everyone. I want you to notice something very powerful about the way David carried himself. David does not lift a hand against Saul! David recognizes that though Saul is truly acting like a tyrannical fool, Saul is still a child of God and called by God as a leader. This is a key point on how to handle yourself around a modern-day Jonah who rejects grace. It's not your job to come against this leader. It's your job to pray for them, love them, and trust that God will take care of whatever correction needs to take place. In Romans 14:4 it says,

Who are you to judge another's servant? To his own master he stands or falls. Indeed, he will be made to stand, for God is able to make him stand.

Sometimes we try to fix problems with our own strength and end up getting in God's way rather than allowing him to work. Now, I'm by no means saying you must stay there and take abuse. I've seen some pretty dramatic scenarios when people are around leaders who have rejected grace and embraced a religious mindset. I'm not encouraging anyone to be a doormat for spiritual abuse at the hand of a leader, but I am encouraging you not to sink down to their level of petty slander.

You can always tell who's in the flesh and who's in the spirit by who's persecuting who. We are not called to attack people. Now, as you take a strong stand for truth, error will be revealed, but our war is not with flesh and blood. Truth in and of itself is confrontational because it declares that there is a right and there is a wrong, but we must take the high road on these issues and not drop down to the level of petty slander.

Stay strong, stand fast in the liberty that Christ has set you free, but don't personally raise your hand against another person or ministry. You maintain your relationship with God and let God sort out the details of correcting his children. Also, each situation is different and we must allow the Holy Spirit to lead us in the details. I know God led me to personally stay in the church I was at after I received the revelation of grace. That pastor regularly attacked me and the message from the pulpit for a solid year. However, I have had other people share with me that God lead them to do something else entirely.

There is no formula on how to handle these modern-day Jonah's. I believe that each of us have the ability to be led and hear God for ourselves better than anyone else. That's why Jesus came to bring the new covenant so we could have a powerful personal relationship with God. However, I promise you that the spirit of God will not lead you to attack or slander any person or ministry on a personal level. When we do things like that we become a part of the problem rather than being a part of the answer.

Listen, I know these situations can be very dramatic and great pain can be inflicted by someone who is operating in a religious mindset and is set on persecuting you. I have experienced these things myself and talked to many people all across the world who have been in similar circumstances. I know you can feel like asking the Lord to call down fire on these people and wipe them off the face of the planet, but let me remind you once again that these people are not the enemy; it's the veil the enemy has used to blind their minds. So in a nutshell, how do you handle these leaders? Pray for them, forgive them, love them, but let God handle them in terms of correcting them. Now, if you have the type of relationship with one of these leaders where you can speak into their lives, then by all means share your heart, but at the end of the day it is between them and God if they choose to receive the revelation or not. God may lead you to stay in their lives or God may lead you to move on, but remember they are not the enemy. Don't lift your hand against them, but be like David and trust that God will take care of his children.

RESTORING THESE LEADERS

God loves these leaders and his desire for them is redemption; many of them have just lost their way or simply do not understand. A few of them choose to reject truth for what they perceive as personal gain, but I believe most are good people like Saul of Tarsus who just don't yet understand.

God may use you to help restore these leaders and bring them into the truth of the gospel. We are called to be minsters of reconciliation and that includes those religious leaders who don't yet understand the magnitude of God's reconciliation in Jesus. All of us are learning and periodically we have found out we were wrong in an area and needed someone to come along and teach us. A great example of this in scripture is Apollos. Let's look at it in Acts 18:24:

Now a certain Jew named Apollos, born at Alexandria, an eloquent man and mighty in the Scriptures, came to Ephesus. This man had been instructed in the way of the Lord; and being fervent in spirit, he spoke and taught accurately the things of the Lord, though he knew only the baptism of John. So, he began to speak boldly in the synagogue. When Aquila and Priscilla heard him, they took him aside and explained to him the way of God more accurately. And when he desired to cross to Achaia, the brethren wrote, exhorting the disciples to receive him; and when he arrived, he greatly helped those who had believed through grace; for he vigorously refuted the Jews publicly, showing from the Scriptures that Jesus is the Christ.

Thank God for people like Aquila and Priscilla, who were kindhearted enough not to condemn or belittle Apollos, but instead took him by the hand and showed him "the way of God more accurately." They could have mocked his limited understanding and closed the door to his heart. They could have called him names and trolled his social media posts. They could have marginalized him and categorized him and set him aside as unenlightened or not as spiritual as them, but instead they saw him through the eyes of the Father and helped him.

Apollos clearly had powerful gifts; the Bible refers to him as "eloquent" and "mighty in the scriptures." As soon as he received the greater revelation, he immediately began to preach Jesus boldly and publicly, showing in the scriptures that he was the Christ. If Aquila and Priscilla were "snobby" with their revelation, none of this would have happened and Apollos would have become more deeply entrenched in error, not fulfilling the true call he had on his life.

I believe God would have raised someone else up to reach him, but how many times have you seen someone condescend and belittle someone else because of their perceived greater revelation? I see that type of scenario take place way too often. You can't disrespect someone and minister to them at the same time. I see some people who have an understanding of the grace of God haughtily persecute and belittle someone who does not; this is a very sad scenario. To be honest, when someone carries the revelation of grace with pride, they don't quite understand it yet. A real revelation of grace will produce love, not pride. We must carry the revelation of grace graciously.

If we can carry ourselves honorably and present the truth in love, we may have opportunities to minister to these leaders who don't yet understand grace. However, if we arrogantly spend our lives disrespecting people who don't believe exactly like us, those opportunities will not be there for us. We should never close the door of ministry through disrespect when we could leave that door open to help a leader understand "the way of God more accurately."

We see this exact scenario happen in Jesus' life and ministry. Most of the religious leaders of the day vehemently opposed Jesus and his teaching, but one leader was curious about the truth. He wasn't willing to go to Jesus in the daytime, when everyone could see, but he was willing to go to Jesus secretly at night. If he had gone in the daytime he would be severely persecuted and even ostracized by his fellow leaders but if he went at night he could check out this truth and ask questions without paying the price of publicly choosing it just yet. We pick up the account in John 3:1–2:

There was a man of the Pharisees named Nicodemus, a ruler of the Jews. This man came to Jesus by night and said to Him, "Rabbi, we know that You are a teacher come from God; for no one can do these signs that You do unless God is with him."

What follows is one of the most engaging and thought-provoking encounters in all of scripture. It is this exchange that produced the most well-known scripture in the entire bible, John 3:16. Nicodemus could not deny the fruit of Jesus' ministry even though he didn't completely understand his message. I believe if we carry the message of grace graciously we leave the door open for Nicodemus to come to us in the night to ask questions about amazing grace. It might not be an actual night meeting per se but it could be a phone call or a private message on social media.

If we can remember that these leaders are not our enemies but that the devil and his lies are our enemy, we can be ministers of reconciliation even to those who persecute us and come against the gospel of grace.

I want to take a look at another figure who was a minister of reconciliation to a very belligerent religious leader of the day. We all know Paul's name, but would we know his name if a man named Ananias didn't have the courage and humility to reach out and minister to him?

Now, I'm sure if Ananias refused to minister to Paul, God would have raised someone else up to fulfill that call, but who knows if Ananias was the first person God came to with this special mission of reconciliation. Also, I know God could have restored him himself, but if you'll notice God likes to work through people. We pick up the account in Acts 9:10:

Now there was a certain disciple at Damascus named Ananias; and to him the Lord said in a vision, "Ananias. "And he said, "Here I am, Lord." So the Lord said to him, "Arise and go to the street called Straight, and inquire at the house of Judas for one called Saul of Tarsus, for behold, he is praying. And in a vision, he has seen a man named Ananias coming in and putting his hand on him, so that he might receive his sight."

Can you imagine receiving this calling from the Lord? God calls you to go and minster to someone who has dedicated their life to destroying everything you believe. At this time, Paul had been hauling off Christians to prison for some time. To me this is the ultimate ministry of reconciliation. We celebrate the prodigal son coming home and being restored to the Father, and so we should, but how glorious would it be for the elder brother to be restored to the Father?

Now, I want to point out that God told Ananias to do this. This wasn't his idea that he concocted in his own mind. In fact, if Ananias had tried to minister to Paul before God had prepared Paul's heart, he could have ended up in prison or dead. God orchestrated this whole event. Let's read on and see what transpires.

Then Ananias answered, "Lord, I have heard from many about this man, how much harm he has done to Your saints in Jerusalem. And here he has authority from the chief priests to bind all who call on Your name."

Understandably, Ananias is a little hesitant, considering the reputation of Paul as a religious leader who persecutes the message of the cross has spread out all over the entire body of Christ. However, God measures him in the next verse.

But the Lord said to him, "Go, for he is a chosen vessel of Mine to bear My name before Gentiles, kings, and the children of Israel. For I will show him how many things he must suffer for My name's sake." And Ananias went his way and entered the house; and laying his hands on him he said, "Brother Saul, the Lord Jesus, who appeared to you on the road as you came, has sent me that you may receive your sight and be filled with the Holy Spirit." Immediately there fell from his eyes something like scales, and he received his sight at once; and he arose and was baptized.

So when he had received food, he was strengthened. Then Saul spent some days with the disciples at Damascus.

How beautiful is this passage of scripture! This is truly an encounter with grace. The most angry, violent legalist in the world meets a man named Ananias, who is filled with grace and truth. I can always tell when someone understands grace because that person is ready to extend grace to someone who doesn't deserve it.

If Ananias had an eye-for-an-eye mentality he would have captured Paul when he was weak and unable to see, but instead he gently restores him. Prays for him, baptizes him, feeds him, and spends time with him. I wonder if Ananias had any idea at the time of the significance of this moment of one-on-one ministry. I mean, two-thirds of the New Testament portion of our Bibles was hanging on this encounter. The book of Romans! The book of Galatians! First Corinthians thirteen, the love chapter! The list goes on and on but the reality is something major is happening here.

The encounter between these two men help shape the world we live in today. Yes, I know Paul had a supernatural encounter with Jesus, but would this encounter be complete without Ananias to follow up and lovingly receive Paul into the fellowship of the body of Christ? Once again, let me ask you a question: Would you be willing to be an Ananias? Would you be willing to humble yourself and courageously extend grace to your undeserving persecutors? Would you be willing to allow God to funnel the ultimate expression of grace through your life to restore a leader who had lost his way?

Timing and leading are everything. We can't do something like this just based on principal and we can't do this just because someone else did it. God prepared Paul's heart and in due time Ananias, led by the spirit, was there to restore this great man of God. However, if Ananias had come to minister to Paul before God had prepared him, the results could have been very ugly.

So please don't think I'm suggesting that you run out and try to convince every legalistic leader you know that grace is God's way. That sounds like a recipe for disaster! However, I do believe that there may potentially be moments like this in our lives.

There may be a time in your journey when you can be an Ananias to a Saul and bring forth tremendous fruit for the kingdom of God. Let's be gracious with grace and walk humbly before our God. We are ministers of recompilation not ministers of separation.

AFTERWORD

AFTERWORD

I ALWAYS FEEL like writing a book is like inviting someone to walk with you for a while. Thank you for going on this journey with me. Thank you for even having the courage to pick up a book with a title like this. I knew when I wrote this book it would have a very specific audience. I didn't write it because I wanted it to be a best seller that would flood our ministry with finances. I wrote it because the Lord dropped the entire thing in my heart one morning when I sat down on the couch.

I have found he is infinitely smarter than I am and his ideas are the best ideas. So I hope this book has ministered to you and given you some insight into the religious mind. I also hope it has birthed compassion in your heart toward these leaders without producing one tiny bit of compromise in your strong stance in amazing grace. I also hope it has given you some practical wisdom on how to handle yourself around leaders who persecute you.

I really wish I had had a book like this to read while I was making the transition from law to grace. But above everything else I hope you take away from this book, I hope you realize that our battle is not with flesh and blood but with the lies of the enemy. Let's stand strong in the gospel of grace but let's remember the word of Jesus as we do.

Matthew 5:9
Blessed are the peacemakers,
For they shall be called sons of God.

There will be a contact page at the end of this book. If there is any way we can help you, please don't hesitate to reach out. You are not alone and there are people who can help.

ABOUT JEREMIAH JOHNSON

Jeremiah is the senior pastor at Grace Point Church in Georgetown, Kentucky. Jeremiah is an author and has a very active traveling ministry. Jeremiah is called to help bring believers into the reality of the new covenant and a deeper understanding of Jesus and his finished work on the cross. Please contact us if you have any questions.

jeremiahjohnsonministries.com
gracepointgeorgetown.com
www.facebook.com/JeremiahJohnsonMinistries
JeremiahJohnsonMinistries@gmail.com
Twitter @gracepoint555

Made in the USA
Coppell, TX
15 February 2024

29079026R00059